MASSACHUSETTS DMV PERMIT TEST MANUAL

Practice and Pass DMV Exams With Over 300 Questions And Answers

Donald Frias

Copyright

This book or any portion thereof may not be reproduced or used in any way whatsoever without the written consent of the Author except for the purpose of brief quotations for book reviews.

Donald Frias ©2018

Disclaimer

This book is intended to be a general guide to help people prepare for and pass their Massachusetts dmv exams.

The author accepts no responsibility for any loss be it personal or financial, as a result for the use or misuse of the information in this book. If you have any doubts or concerns after reading this book, please reach out to the author or anybody of relevant authority.

© Donald Frias

Table Of Content

GENERAL QUESTIONS

76 QUESTIONS

DEFENSIVE DRIVING

56 QUESTIONS

ROAD SIGNS

80 QUESTIONS

TRAFFIC CONTROL

75 QUESTIONS

SPECIAL DRIVING CONDITION

38 QUESTIONS

ANSWERS PAGE

Study Guide

Testing Strategy

GENERAL QUESTIONS
76 QUESTIONS

1. When making a turn, you must _____ your speed.

    A. Increase

    B. Maintain

    C. Vary

    D. Reduce

2. When you drive in heavy fog during daylight hours you should drive with your

    A. Headlights off.

    B. Parking lights on.

    C. Headlights on low beam.

    D. Headlights on high beam.

3. This sign means?

   A. Warning of a winding road ahead.

   B. Warning of a right curve ahead.

   C. Warning of merging traffic to the right.

   D. Warning of a right turn ahead.

4. Which of these vehicles must always stop before crossing railroad tracks?

   A. Tank trucks marked with hazardous materials placards.

   B. Pickup trucks towing a boat trailer.

   C. Any vehicle with 3 or more axles or weighing more than 4,000 pounds.

5. As you drive, you are required to stop your vehicle:

   A. At an intersection with a stop sign

   B. Where there is a red light

   C. When a traffic officer orders you to stop

   D. All of the above

6. Choose the best answer for driving on a slipper surface with snow or ice.

>A. Allow less space than usual between you and the car in front of you

>B. Use your parking lights

>C. Pump your brakes to keep them from freezing

>D. Drive slowly to avoid sudden turns or stops

7. It is important to slow down:

>A. On narrow or winding roads

>B. At intersections or railroad crossings

>C. When the road is wet or slippery

>D. All of the above

8. Compared to driving during the day, driving at night is:

    A. Less dangerous

    B. No more of less dangerous

    C. More dangerous

    D. Easier on your eyes

9. This sign means?

    A. A sharp left curve warning.

    B. A sharp right curve or turn.

    C. V intersection ahead.

    D. 2 Lane traffic ahead.

10. What happens to your driver`s license if you refuse to take a chemical test (breath or blood)

    A. There is no evidence to find you guilty of drunk driving.

    B. You cannot be arrested for drunk driving.

    C. Your driver`s license will be taken away.

    D. None of these choices.

11. If your brake pedal suddenly sinks to the floor, you should first

   A. Try to pump it to build up the pressure.

   B. Shift into neutral and shut the engine off.

   C. Try to raise it by hooking your toe under it.

   D. Apply the parking brake hard to stop the car.

12. Roadways are the most slippery:

   A. During a heavy downpour.

   B. After it has been raining for awhile.

   C. The first rain after a dry spell.

13. If you have a tire blowout, you should:

   A. Allow the steering wheel to move freely

   B. Let the car slow to a stop

   C. Continue driving until you reach a garage

   D. Brake hard to stop the car immediately

14. To prepare for anything coming up in the road ahead, you should:

>A. Continually scan the entire road and roadsides

>B. Stare straight ahead at all times

>C. Drive with your left foot resting lightly on the brake pedal

>D. Maintain focus toward the middle of the road

15. This sign means?

>A. Advance warning of a cross intersection.

>B. X intersection ahead warning sign.

>C. No right turn warning.

>D. Railroad crossing ahead warning sign.

16. This sign means?

    A. Pedestrian crossing ahead.

    B. School advance warning, you are entering a school zone.

    C. Pedestrians only, no vehicle traffic.

    D. Pedestrians ahead warning sign.

17. When faced with one oncoming car to the left and a bicyclist to the right, you should:

    A. Pull onto the shoulder

    B. Split the difference

    C. Let the car pass and then pass the bike

    D. Pass the bike quickly

18. Preparing to smoke and smoking while driving:

    A. Do not affect driving abilities

    B. Help maintain driver alertness

    C. Are distracting activities

    D. Are not distracting activities

19. At what distance should you stop when you see active crossing devices at the railroad crossing?

    A. A maximum of 50 feet and a minimum of 15 feet from the nearest railroad track

    B. At least 30 feet but not more than 100 feet from the nearest track

    C. At least 30 feet but not more than 50 feet from the nearest track

20. A bicyclist differs from a motorist in that he is not required to

    A. Obey the same traffic laws.

    B. Signal all turns.

    C. Report accidents resulting in serious injury.

    D. Insure the bicycle.

21. A diamond-shaped sign is a

    A. Road hazard sign.

    B. Interstate route sign.

    C. School crossing sign.

    D. Speed limit sign.

22. This sign means?

   A. No left turn.

   B. No u-turn.

   C. No right turn.

   D. No turn on red.

23. The zero tolerance law reduced the blood alcohol content (bac) from .08% to ____ for drivers under 21 to be charged with driving under the influence.

   A. .02%

   B. .05%

   C. .07%

   D. .00%

24. If you drive faster than other vehicles on a road with one lane in each direction and continually pass the other cars, you will:

   A. Get you to your destination much faster and safer.

   B. Increase your chances of an accident.

   C. Help prevent traffic congestion.

25. For a first conviction for driving under the influence at any blood alcohol concentration level, you could:

   A. Lose your license for up to 5 years

   B. Be required to conduct a public education class on the dangers of drunk driving

   C. Be required to drive with a restricted occupational license

   D. Pay a fine of at least $300

26. A red and white triangular sign at an intersection means

   A. Slow down if an emergency vehicle is approaching.

   B. Look both ways as you cross the intersection.

   C. Always come to a full stop at the intersection.

   D. Slow down and be prepared to stop if necessary.

27. If you are driving and a dust storm blows across the freeway causing reduced visibility, you should reduce your speed and turn on your:

   A. Emergency flashers.

   B. Parking lights.

C. Head lights.

D. Horn

28. What does a slow moving vehicle emblem look like

    A. A square red sign.

    B. A round green sign.

    C. A diamond-shaped yellow sign.

    D. A triangular orange sign.

29. You must use your headlights when other vehicles are not visible from _____ feet away.

    A. 1000

    B. 1500

    C. 1800

    D. 1200

30. The driver`s right hand and arm are extended upward. This hand signal means that the driver plans to

    A. Turn left.

    B. Turn right.

    C. Come to a stop.

    D. Go straight ahead.

31. Which of these can help to maximize fuel economy?

    A - Cruise control

    B - Air suspension

    C - Re-grooved Tire

    D - Diff-lock

32. A laminated windscreen is one which

    A - will not shatter

    B - does not mist up

    C - has a plastic layer

    D - cuts down on glare

33. You are driving a long vehicle.

    Before turning left onto a main road you should be ESPECIALLY careful of

    2 answers required

    A - cyclists alongside you on the left

    B - motorcyclists alongside you on the left

    C - motorcyclists coming from your left

    D - cyclists coming from your left

34. A bus driver MUST not drive while

>3 answers required

A - issuing tickets

B - the doors are open

C - wearing sunglasses

D - giving change

E - passengers are standing

F - luggage is being carried

35. What basic rule applies when you're using a Truck?

A - Use the lane that has the least traffic

B - Keep to the left-hand lane unless overtaking

C - Overtake on the side that's clearest

D - Try to keep above 50 mph to prevent congestion

36. When should you use hazard warning lights?

A - To warn other drivers that you are towing

B - Approaching queuing traffic on a Truck

C - When parked illegally on a busy road

D - To thank a driver for giving way to you

37. Overloading your vehicle can seriously affect the

   2 answers required

   A - gearbox

   B - steering

   C - handling

   D - battery life

   E - journey time

38. An emergency situation has arisen. For safety reasons you will need to exceed the normal drivers' hours under EC rules. You should

   A - continue with the same tachograph chart and write an explanation on the back

   B - remove the tachograph chart and make a manual record of the rest of the journey

   C - continue; there is no need to give anexplanation

   D - remove the tachograph chart and inform your employer of the reason

39. You are about to overtake a motorcyclist. They look over their right shoulder.

   It is most likely that

   A - the rider intends moving to the right

B - something has fallen from the machine

C - the drive chain is slack

D - the rear tyre is flat

40. What could prevent air pressure building up in an air brake system

   in cold frosty weather?

   A - Moisture in the air may form bubbles in the brake fluid

   B - The air will contract, reducing the pressure

   C - The dampness may cause valves to rust

   D - Moisture drawn in with the air may freeze and cause a blockage

41. Your vehicle has collided with a railway bridge.

   You must telephone the railway authority to inform them of the

   3 answers required

   A - damage caused

   B - type of bridge

   C - vehicle height

   D - bridge number

E - vehicle number

F - bridge location

42. A long, heavily laden Truck is taking a long time to overtake you.

    What should you do?

    A - Speed up

    B - Slow down

    C - Hold your speed

    D - Change direction

43. You wish to turn right ahead. Why should you take up the correct position in good time?

    A - To allow other drivers to pull out in front of you

    B - To give a better view into the road that you are joining

    C - To help other road users know what you intend to do

    D - To allow drivers to pass you on the right

44. A driver is applying for a LGV or PCV license for the first time. They need UNCORRECTED visual acuity in each eye of at least

    A - 3/60

B - 6/9

C - 6/12

D - 9/60

45. What's the minimum time gap you should leave when following a vehicle on a wet road?

    A - One second

    B - Two seconds

    C - Three seconds

    D - Four seconds

46. You are at the front of a queue of traffic waiting to turn right into a side road.

    Why is it important to check your right mirror just before turning?

    A - To look for pedestrians about to cross

    B - To check for overtaking vehicles

    C - To make sure the side road is clear

    D - To check for emerging traffic

47. Because of its size and design a large vehicle will have

    A - less blind spots than smaller vehicles

    B - more blind spots than smaller vehicles

C - the same blind spots as smaller vehicles

D - no blind spots at all

48. The audible warning device is operating as you reverse.

   You should be

   A - relying on a clear path behind

   B - expecting others to be aware of your course

   C - taking continuous, all-round observation

   D - concentrating solely on your blind areas

49. At the end of your working week you have driven a total of 56 hours.

   What is the maximum number of hours that you can

   drive in the following week under EC rules?

   A - 34

   B - 36

   C - 38

   D – 40

50. A pelican crossing that crosses the road in a STRAIGHT line

and has a central island must be treated as

A - one crossing in daylight only

B - one complete crossing

C - two separate crossings

D - two crossings during darkness

51. At a traffic incident a casualty is unconscious.

    Which THREE of the following should you check urgently?

    3 answers required

    A - Circulation

    B - Airway

    C - Shock

    D - Breathing

    E - Broken bones

52. Which three of the following could cause unnecessary pollution to the environment?

    3 answers required

    A - Excessive exhaust fumes

    B - Regular servicing

    C - Vehicles driven poorly

D - Poorly maintained vehicles

E - High level exhaust systems

53. You are behind a large vehicle.

How can you improve your view ahead?

A - Stay further back

B - Move over to the right

C - Move over to the left

D - Overtake as soon as you can

54. Codes are shown on the side walls of bus and Truck Tire.

What do these refer to?

A - Tread pattern

B - Minimum temperature

C - Maximum load

D - Running pressure

55. As a bus driver your main responsibility is

A - the safety and comfort of your passengers

B - keeping to a strict timetable

C - the collecting of fares

D - the issuing of tickets

56. You are driving a bus in hot weather.

    May the passenger door be left open to let fresh air in?

    A - Yes, this is normal practice

    B - No, unless all passengers are seated

    C - Yes, unless carrying school children

    D - No, this is not allowed

57. Why have 'red routes' been introduced in major cities?

    A - To raise the speed limits

    B - To help the traffic flow

    C - To provide better parking

    D - To allow lorries to load more freely

58. Diamond-shaped signs give instructions to drivers of

    A - lorries

B - trams

C - buses

D – tractors

59. What does this sign mean?

A - Stop only to pick up passengers

B - No stopping at any time

C - Stop only to set down passengers

D - No stopping at peak times

60. You are delivering a load of building materials on pallets.

Before unloading what should you ensure FIRST?

A - The engine is switched off

B - You are parked on firm level ground

C - The stabilizing legs are lowered

D - You have warning cones set out

61. You are unable to allow a person in a wheelchair to enter your bus.

> What would be the reason for this?
>
> A - Passengers are standing in a wheelchair space and cannot move elsewhere
>
> B - You will take time to load the wheelchair and fall behind schedule
>
> C - The wheelchair passenger will have to stand up
>
> D - You cannot fold down the wheelchair

62. At the scene of an accident a person has become hysterical.

> You should calm them by
>
> A - leaving them to quietly recover
>
> B - shouting at them loudly
>
> C - giving them a hot drink
>
> D - talking quietly and firmly to them

63. Many sleep-related vehicle incidents (SRVIs) occur at work.

> Men are more likely than women to be involved.
>
> Between what ages are men most at risk?

A - 30 years and under

B - 31 - 45 years

C - 46 - 59 years

D - 60 years and over

64. You arrive at the scene of an accident. It has just happened, and someone is unconscious. Which of the following should be given urgent priority to help them? 3 answers required

    A - Clear the airway and keep it open

    B - Try to get them to drink water

    C - Check that they are breathing

    D - Look for any witnesses

    E - Stop any heavy bleeding

    F - Take the numbers of vehicles involved

65. You want to turn right at a roundabout marked with two right-turn lanes. There is ample room for your vehicle in either lane. You should

    A - use the right-hand of the two lanes

    B - use the left-hand of the two lanes

    C - use the left-hand lane then move to the right as you enter the roundabout

D - use the right-hand lane then move to the left as you enter the roundabout

66. You are two and a half times over the legal alcohol limit. You are disqualified from driving. Before regaining your license who will you have to satisfy that you do NOT have an alcohol problem?

    A - The local hospital

    B - Drivers' Medical Branch, DVLA

    C - Alcoholics Anonymous

    D - Vehicle and Operator Services Agency

67. You are driving a high-sided vehicle. You are about to drive over a high suspension bridge. What in particular do you need to be aware of?

    A - The swaying of the bridge

    B - The width of the lanes

    C - The effect of strong crosswinds

    D - The overhanging bridge cables

68. You're driving a slow-moving vehicle on a narrow, winding road. What should you do?

    A - Keep well out to stop vehicles overtaking dangerously

    B - Wave following vehicles past you if you think they can overtake quickly

    C - Pull in when you can, to let following vehicles overtake

    D - Give a left signal when it's safe for vehicles to overtake you

69. You are driving through a tunnel. Your vehicle breaks down. What should you do?

    A - Switch on hazard warning lights

    B - Remain in your vehicle

    C - Wait for the police to find you

    D - Rely on CCTV cameras seeing you

70. While you're driving in fog, it becomes necessary to use front fog lights. What should you remember?

    A - Only use them in heavy traffic conditions

    B - Don't use them on Trucks

    C - Only use them on dual carriageways

    D - Switch them off when visibility improves

71. You are driving on a Truck. A moving Truck just ahead of you switches on its hazard warning lights. What does this mean?

    A - There are speed cameras ahead

    B - The Truck is about to change lanes

C - The Truck is leaving the Truck

D - Traffic further ahead may be stopping

72. You are driving on a main road. You intend to turn right into a side road.

Just before turning you should

A - adjust your interior mirror

B - flash your headlights

C - steer over to the left

D - check for traffic overtaking on your right

73. How could you save fuel when driving?

3 answers required

A - By reducing overall speed

B - By braking as late as you can

C - By planning routes to avoid congestion

D - By having properly inflated Tire

E - By extending vehicles' service times

74. When roping down a load on your Truck what is the best knot to use?

A - A dolly knot

B - A reef knot

C - A slip knot

D - A bow-line knot

75. When planning your route which of the following should be taken into consideration?

    3 answers required

    A - Any weight restrictions

    B - Any height restrictions

    C - Any speed restrictions

    D - Any parking restrictions

    E - Any width restrictions

76. Which of the following would be most affected by a vehicle with faulty suspension?

    2 answers required

    A - Underground pipes

    B - Road surfaces

    C - Tyre pressures

    D - Road tunnels

    E - Overhead gantries

DEFENSIVE DRIVING
56 QUESTIONS

1. When sharing the road with a truck, it is important to remember that, in general, trucks:

    A. Take longer distances than cars to stop

    B. Require less time to pass on a downgrade than cars

    C. Require less turning radius than cars

    D. Require less time to pass on an incline than cars

2. When entering a freeway:

    A. Vehicles on the freeway must always yield the right-of-way to vehicles that are entering the freeway.

    B. You must yield the right-of-way to vehicles already on the freeway.

    C. Increase your speed even if the way is not clear.

    D. You must always drive at the same speed as the rest of the traffic.

3. When driving on a freeway entrance ramp, you should look for a gap in freeway traffic by:

A. Looking in the inside rearview mirror only

B. Looking in the side view mirror only

C. Looking in both rearview and side view mirrors

D. Looking in your mirrors and turning your head to look over your shoulder

4. You need to use extra caution when driving near a pedestrian using a white cane because:

    A. He or she is deaf

    B. He or she has a mental disability

    C. He or she is blind

    D. He or she has a walking problem

5. At night, it is hardest to see:

    A. Road signs

    B. Pedestrians

    C. Other motorists

    D. Street lights

6. The four-second rule refers to how one should:

    A. Yield to other cars

B. Turn at stop signs

C. Follow another car

D. Cross an intersection

7. U-turns in residential districts are legal:

A. On a one-way street on a green arrow.

B. When there are no vehicles approaching nearby.

C. Across two sets of solid double, yellow lines.

8. The only time you do not have to stop for a school bus whose red lights are flashing and stop arm is extended is when you:

A. Are driving on the opposite side of a divided highway

B. Are behind the bus

C. See no children present

D. Can safely pass on the left

9. The law gives _____ the right of way at intersections.

   A. No one

   B. Drivers turning left

   C. Drivers going straight

   D. Drivers turning right

10. Seat belts can be most effective as injury preventive devices when they are worn by

    A. The person driving the car.

    B. Passengers when they are on a long drive.

    C. All occupants of a car being driven on an expressway.

    D. Passengers and the driver whenever they are in the car.

11. When exiting a highway, you should slow down:

    A. On the main road, just before the exit lane

    B. Once you see the toll booth

    C. Once you have moved into the exit lane

    D. When you first see the exit sign

12. You can park and leave your car

   A. In a tunnel.

   B. 30 feet from a railroad crossing.

   C. Between a safety zone and the curb.

   D. None of the above.

13. When a school bus has its lights flashing and its stop arm extended, you must:

   A. Stop at least 10 feet away from the bus

   B. Pass if children have exited the bus

   C. Stop if the bus is on the opposite side of a barrier

   D. Drive slowly by the bus

14. Drivers who eat and drink while driving:

   A. Have no driving errors

   B. Have trouble driving slow

   C. Are better drivers because they are not hungry

   D. Have trouble controlling their vehicles

15. When passing a bicyclist, you should:

   A. Blast your horn to alert the bicyclist

   B. Move as far left as possible

C. Remain in the center of the lane

D. Put on your four-way flashers

16. Who must yield when a driver is turning and a pedestrian is crossing without a traffic light?

    A. Whoever started last

    B. The driver

    C. Whoever is slower

    D. The pedestrian

17. To turn left on multi-lane streets and highways, you should start from:

    A. The middle of the intersection

    B. The right lane

    C. The left lane

    D. Any lane

18. Always use your seat belt:

    A. Unless the vehicle was built before 1978.

    B. Unless you are in a limousine.

    C. When the vehicle is equipped with seat belt

19. You drive defensively when you:

> A. Always put one car length between you and the car ahead.
>
> B. Look only at the car in front of you while driving.
>
> C. Keep your eyes moving to look for possible hazards.

20. It is best to keep a space cushion:

> A. Only in back of your vehicle
>
> B. Only on the left and right side of your vehicle
>
> C. Only in front of the vehicle
>
> D. On all sides of the vehicle

21. Which of the following statements about blind spots is true?

> A. They are eliminated if you have one outside mirror on each side of the vehicle.
>
> B. Large trucks have bigger blind spots than most passenger vehicles.
>
> C. Blind spots can be checked by looking in your rear view mirrors.

22. When entering a highway from an entrance ramp, you should generally:

>A. Enter above the speed of traffic to get ahead

>B. Enter slowly to avoid other vehicles

>C. Stop first, then slowly enter traffic

>D. Accelerate to the speed of traffic

23. Allowing a space cushion is important because it:

>A. Prevents distractions from other vehicles

>B. Allows you time to react to situations

>C. Keeps traffic flowing at a safe pace

>D. Keeps other drivers alert

24. One of the rules of defensive driving is

>A. Look straight ahead as you drive.

>B. Stay alert and keep your eyes moving.

>C. Expect that other drivers will make up for your errors.

>D. Be confident that you can avoid danger at the last minute.

25. When passing on a multi-lane highway:

    A. Be sure the passing lane is clear

    B. Pass only on the right

    C. Watch for oncoming traffic

    D. There is no need to signal

26. To make a right turn at the corner, you:

    A. May not enter the bicycle lane.

    B. Should only merge into the bicycle lane if you stop before turning.

    C. Must merge into the bicycle lane before turning.

27. Drivers entering a roundabout or traffic circle:

    A. Must stop before entering

    B. Must yield to drivers in the roundabout or traffic circle

    C. Have the right of way if they arrive first

    D. Have the right of way if there are two lanes

28. Under normal conditions, a safe following distance between your car and the car ahead is:

    A. Fifty feet.

    B. One car length.

    C. Three second behind the vehicle you follow

    D. One hundred feet

29. On two-lane, two-way streets or highways, you should start left turns:

    A. Close to the center line

    B. Close to the outside line

    C. In the center of the lane

    D. Anywhere in the lane

30. teenage drivers are more likely to be involved in a crash when:

    A. They are driving with their pet as a passenger

    B. They are driving with adult passengers

    C. They are driving with teenage passengers

    D. They are driving without any passengers

31. When you are merging onto the freeway, you should be driving:

>A. At or near the same speed as the traffic on the freeway.

>B. 5 to 10 MPH slower than the traffic on the freeway.

>C. The posted speed limit for traffic on the freeway.

32. Collisions can happen more often when:

>A. All vehicles are traveling about the same speed.

>B. One lane of traffic is traveling faster than the other lanes.

>C. One vehicle is traveling faster or slower than the flow of traffic.

33. On long trips you can prevent drowsiness by

>A. Turning on your car radio.

>B. Slowing down so you can react better.

>C. Stopping at regular intervals for a rest.

>D. Moving your eyes from side to side as you drive.

34. To pass a slower-moving vehicle on a two-lane road you must:

> A. Not cross the center line
>
> B. Flash your lights to oncoming traffic
>
> C. Use the shoulder
>
> D. Use that lane that belongs to oncoming traffic

35. When you drive through an area where children are playing, you should expect them:

> A. To know when it is safe to cross
>
> B. To stop at the curb before crossing the street
>
> C. To run out in front of you without looking
>
> D. Not to cross unless they are with an adult

36. When traveling behind a motorcycle:

> A. Allow a following distance of at least 2 car lengths
>
> B. Allow at least 2 seconds of following distance
>
> C. Allow at least 4 seconds of following distance

D. Allow a following distance of at least 4 motorcycle lengths

37. If you are following a truck that swings left before making a right turn at an intersection, you should remember that it is very dangerous to:

   A. Try to squeeze between the truck and curb to make a right turn

   B. Apply your brakes until the truck has completed the turn

   C. Violate the 4-second following distance rule

   D. Honk your horn at the truck driver

38. Preparing to smoke and smoking while driving:

   A. Do not affect driving abilities

   B. Help maintain driver alertness

   C. Are distracting activities

   D. Are not distracting activities

39. The most important thing to remember about speed management and curves is to:

   A. Drive at the posted speed limit as you enter the curve, then slow down at the sharpest part of the curve

   B. Slow down before you enter the curve

C. Accelerate gently before you enter the curve

D. Drive at the posted speed limit of the roadway, before, throughout, and after the curve

40. If you want to get off from a freeway, but you missed your exit, you should:

> A. Go to the next exit, and get off the freeway there
>
> B. Make a U-turn through the median
>
> C. Pull onto the shoulder and back your car to the exit
>
> D. Flag down a police officer for an escort back to your exit

41. When no signs, signals, or police tell you what to do at an intersection, the law states that:

> A. Drivers on the right must yield to drivers on the left
>
> B. There are no laws stating who must yield
>
> C. Drivers going straight must yield to drivers turning left at the intersection
>
> D. Drivers turning left must yield to drivers going straight through the intersection

42. Highway hypnosis is a driver condition that can result from:

    A. Staring at the roadway for long periods of time

    B. Frequent rest stops

    C. Too much sleep the night before your trip

    D. Short trips on expressways

43. To avoid last minute moves, you should be looking down the road to where your vehicle will be in about ____.

    A. 5 to 10 seconds

    B. 10 to 15 seconds

    C. 15 to 20 seconds

44. If you stop at a railroad crossing with more than one track:

    A. Wait until you have a clear view of all tracks

    B. Stop on the railroad track and watch for another train

    C. Go through as soon as the train passes

    D. Go through when one of the tracks is free

45. If you are driving behind a motorcycle, you must:

   A. Allow the motorcycle to use a complete lane

   B. Drive on the shoulder beside the motorcycle

   C. Allow the motorcycle to use only half a lane

   D. Pass in the same lane where the motorcycle is driving

46. After a train has passed, you should:

   A. Check again for approaching trains and proceed with caution

   B. Wait for a green light

   C. Proceed across the tracks

   D. Blow horn and proceed

47. A safe speed to drive your car

   A. Is the posted speed limit.

   B. Is less than the posted speed limit.

   C. Depends on the weather and road conditions.

   D. Depends on the mechanical skill of the driver.

48. When driving near a blind pedestrian who is carrying a white cane or using a guide dog, you should:

    A. Slow down and be prepared to stop

    B. Take the right-of-way

    C. Proceed normally

    D. Drive away quickly

49. Minimum speed signs are designed to

    A. Keep traffic flowing smoothly.

    B. Show current local road conditions.

    C. Test future traffic signal needs.

    D. Assure pedestrian safety.

50. You are waiting to turn left at a multilane intersection, and opposing traffic is blocking your view, you should:

    A. Accelerate rapidly when the first lane you need to cross is clear

    B. Wait until you can see all the lanes you need to cross before going ahead with your turn

    C. Wait for the opposing driver to wave you across the intersection

D. Edge your car into each lane of opposing traffic as soon as it clears

51. When a truck driver behind you wants to pass your vehicle, your speed should:

    A. Remain steady or decrease

    B. Change lanes

    C. Change

    D. Increase

52. On a two-lane road, you may pass another vehicle on the right when:

    A. Driving on a single lane entrance ramp

    B. The driver you are passing is travelling slower than the posted speed limit

    C. Never

    D. The driver you are passing is making a left turn

53. An orange triangle on the back of a vehicle indicates that vehicle:

    A. Carries radioactive materials

    B. Takes wide turns

    C. Travels at slower speeds than normal traffic

    D. Makes frequent stops

54. Your lane position should _____

    A. increase wind blast from other vehicles.

    B. protect your lane from other drivers.

    C. decrease your ability to see and be seen.

    D. all the above

55. These pavement markings tell you that at the intersection ahead:

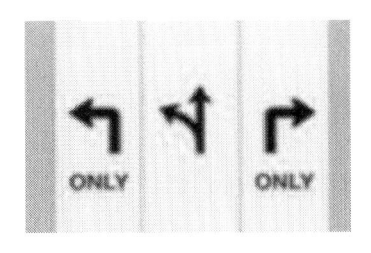

    A. Center lane traffic may go straight or turn left

    B. You can only turn right from the center lane

    C. The center lane mergers into one lane

    D. Center lane traffic must turn left

56. At an intersection with a stop sign, you should stop and:

    A. Check your rearview mirror for cars tailgating

    B. Go when the vehicle ahead of you goes

C. Look right first, then left, then right again

D. Look both ways ahead and ensure it is clear and safe before moving off.

      Answer D

ROAD SIGNS
80 QUESTIONS

1. This warning sign means?

    A. Left curve ahead warning.

    B. Merging traffic from the right.

    C. Hairpin curve ahead, extreme right curve.

    D. Right turn ahead warning.

2. This warning sign means?

    A. Right lane stays to the right, left lane stays to the left.

    B. Keep to the right, merging traffic ahead.

    C. Keep to the left, merging traffic ahead.

    D. Traffic is permitted to pass on either side of an island or obstruction.

3. This sign means?

    A. Highway exit only.

    B. One lane traffic, keep to the right.

    C. Traffic is prohibited from entering a restricted roadway.

    D. Road closed, construction ahead.

4. This road sign means:

    A. No U-turn.

    B. Curve.

    C. Turn right or left.

    D. Traffic flows only in the direction of the arrow.

5. This sign means

   A. Divided highway ahead.

   B. One-way traffic ahead.

   C. Four-lane highway ahead.

   D. Divided highway ends.

6. This warning sign means?

   A. Right lane stays to the right, left lane stays to the left.

   B. Keep to the right, merging traffic ahead.

   C. Keep to the left, merging traffic ahead.

   D. Traffic is permitted to pass on either side of an island or obstruction.

7. What type of sign is this?

    A. State route sign.

    B. U. S. route sign.

    C. County route sign.

    D. Interstate route sign.

8. This sign means?

    A. General information sign for a library.

    B. General information sign for a bus stop.

    C. General information sign for a school.

    D. General information sign for a park.

9. This sign means?

   A. No motor vehicles allowed.

   B. No pedestrian crossing.

   C. Pedestrian crossing.

   D. School crossing.

10. This warning sign means?

    A. Winding road ahead.

    B. The road ahead curves sharply right, then left.

    C. The road ahead turns sharply left.

    D. The road ahead curves sharply left, then right.

11. This sign means

A. Slow down if an emergency vehicle is approaching.

B. Look both ways as you cross the intersection.

C. Always come to a full stop at the intersection.

D. Slow down and be prepared to stop if necessary.

12. This sign means?

A. No left turn.

B. No u-turn.

C. No right turn.

D. No turn on red.

13. This sign means?

A. Merging traffic from the right.

B. Winding road, use caution.

C. Slippery when wet, use caution.

D. Sharp left curve then right curve, use caution.

14. This road sign means:

A. Right lane ends soon, merge left.

B. Soft shoulders.

C. Low place in the road.

D. Lane ends soon, merge right

15. This sign means

A. Continue at your current speed.

B. You must stop ahead.

C. Speeding is not allowed.

D. There is a traffic signal ahead.

16. This sign means?

A. Maximum legal speed is 50 mph in ideal conditions.

B. Maximum legal speed is 50 mph in all weather conditions.

C. Minimum legal speed is 50 mph in ideal conditions.

D. Minimum legal speed is 50 mph in all weather conditions.

17. This sign means

A. One-way traffic

B. Intersection ahead.

C. Merging traffic from the right.

D. Highway curves ahead.

18. This sign means?

A. Advance warning of a low speed sharp left curve.

B. Road curves right, then turns left.

C. Advance warning of a winding road.

D. Advance warning of a right curve.

19. A white painted curb means:

> A. Loading zone for freight or passengers.
>
> B. Loading zone for passengers or mail only.
>
> C. Loading zone for freight only.

20. This warning sign means.

> A. Reverse curve ahead.
>
> B. One-way traffic ahead.
>
> C. A divided highway ends ahead.
>
> D. A divided highway begins ahead.

21. What type of sign is this?

> A. State route sign.
>
> B. U. S. route sign.

C. County route sign.

D. Interstate route sign.

22. This sign means?

A. Warning sign for truck ramp.

B. Warning sign for draw bridge ahead.

C. Warning sign for hill ahead.

D. No trucks warning sign.

23. This sign means?

A. Warning of divided highway ends ahead.

B. Warning of divided highway begins ahead.

C. Two way traffic advance warning.

D. Winding road advance warning.

24. This sign means?

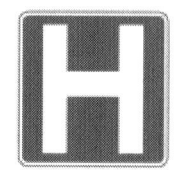

A. Route H highway sign.

B. General service sign for a highway.

C. General service sign for a hotel.

D. General service sign for a hospital.

25. This sign means

A. Trucks under 18,000 lbs. allowed.

B. Hill ahead.

C. Truck stop ahead.

D. No trucks allowed

26. This warning sign means?

A. This road or street terminates ahead.

B. Do not enter, wrong way.

C. Two-way traffic ends ahead.

D. Wrong way, turn around.

27. This sign means?

A. Come to a complete stop, proceed only when safe to do so.

B. Slow down and yield to oncoming traffic

C. Stop only to avoid an accident

D. Slow down and proceed if traffic allows.

28. What type of sign is this?

A. Interstate route sign.

B. County route sign.

C. State route sign.

D. U. S. route sign.

29. This sign means?

   A. General information sign for an aircraft manufacturing plant.

   B. No fly zone ahead.

   C. General information sign for an airport.

   D. Low flying aircraft warning.

30. The correct hand signal for stopping is:

   A. Right hand and arm pointing downward.

   B. Left hand and arm pointing straight out.

   C. Left hand and arm pointing downward.

   D. Left hand and arm pointing upward.

31. This sign means?

   A. T-Road intersection ahead.

B. A two-way intersection ahead.

C. A four-way intersection ahead.

D. Side road intersection ahead.

32. This sign means?

    A. Narrow bridge warning.

    B. Merging traffic from the right.

    C. Left lane ends ahead.

    D. Soft shoulder warning.

33. This sign means?

    A. Max speed 50 mph, minimum speed 30 mph in all conditions.

    B. Speed limit is 50 mph, minimum fine of $50 for violations.

    C. Max speed 50 mph, minimum speed 30 mph in ideal conditions.

D. Speed limit is 50 mph, minimum fine of $30 for violations.

34. This warning sign means?

A. Winding road ahead, begins with a curve to the right.

B. The road curves to the left then to the right.

C. Winding road ahead, begins with a curve to the left.

D. Slippery when wet.

35. This road sign means:

A. You may turn during the red light.

B. Pass only in the right lane.

C. One way street.

D. Do not turn during the red light.

36. This sign means?

    A. U-turn is prohibited.

    B. No left lane.

    C. Left lane ends.

    D. No left turn.

37. This sign means?

    A. Two way traffic warning.

    B. Warning for 2 lane highway.

    C. Left lane ends ahead.

    D. Right lane ends ahead.

38. This sign means

A. Merging traffic is approaching from the right.

B. Winding road ahead.

C. Right lane ends ahead, stay to the left.

D. Divided highway ahead.

39. This sign means?

A. No playing in the street.

B. No parking allowed.

C. No passing allowed.

D. No pedestrian traffic.

40. This warning sign means?

A. U-turns allowed ahead.

B. Left curve ahead.

C. Circular intersection ahead.

D. Three-way intersection ahead.

41. This warning sign means?

A. Road striping ahead.

B. Utility crew ahead.

C. Children`s playground ahead.

D. Road maintenance crew ahead.

42. This road sign means:

A. Warning of a hazard.

B. Yield right-of-way.

C. Railroad crossing.

D. Speed limit.

43. This sign means?

A. Four-way intersection ahead.

B. Side road intersection ahead.

C. Intersection warning ahead, roadway ends, must turn right or left.

D. Y intersection ahead.

44. This sign means?

A. Warning that a stop sign is ahead.

B. Forward traffic is not allowed.

C. Wrong way, do not enter.

D. A warning to stop right away.

45. This sign means?

   A. A sharp left curve warning.

   B. A sharp right curve or turn.

   C. V intersection ahead.

   D. 2 Lane traffic ahead.

46. This warning sign means?

   A. Pavement ends ahead.

   B. Lane ends ahead.

   C. Road construction ahead.

   D. Road closed ahead.

47. This sign means?

A. Warning of a winding road ahead.

B. Warning of a right curve ahead.

C. Warning of merging traffic to the right.

D. Warning of a right turn ahead.

48. If you see orange construction signs and cones on a freeway, you must:

    A. Slow down because the lane ends ahead.

    B. Be prepared for workers and equipment ahead.

    C. Change lanes and maintain your current speed.

49. This sign means

    A. All traffic turn left.

    B. No left turn.

    C. No U-turn.

    D. Truck route to the left.

50. This sign means

A. Don't drink if you are going to drive.

B. Slippery when wet.

C. Road curves ahead.

D. You are approaching a hill.

51. This warning sign means?

A. Pavement ends ahead.

B. Ahead is a sharp depression in the profile of the road.

C. Ahead is a narrow bridge warning.

D. Ahead is a sharp rise in the profile of the road.

52. This road sign means:

A. Church.

B. First aid station.

C. Four-way intersection.

D. Railroad crossing.

53. This sign means?

A. No hunting allowed.

B. Wildlife reserve area.

C. Deer crossing ahead.

D. State park area.

54. This sign means?

A. No u-turn.

B. No right turn.

C. No turn on red.

D. No left turn.

55. Two sets of solid, double, yellow lines that are two or more feet apart:

A. May be crossed to enter or exit a private driveway.

B. May not be crossed for any reason.

C. Should be treated as a separate traffic lane.

56. This sign means?

A. A flagger is stationed ahead to control road users.

B. End of road construction.

C. Road construction detour to the left.

D. Road construction detour to the right.

57. This sign means?

    A. General service sign for a hospital.

    B. General service sign for a doctor's office.

    C. General service sign for a pharmacy.

    D. General service sign for parking.

58. This warning sign means?

    A. Merging traffic entering from the left.

    B. Merging traffic entering from the right.

    C. Two lane traffic ahead.

    D. Intersection warning ahead.

59. What does this sign mean?

A. A truck is 500 feet ahead of you.

B. Slow down for the truck ahead.

C. A farm vehicle, or tractor, is 500 feet ahead of you.

D. Caution and keep a 500 foot distance between yourself and the farm vehicle ahead of you.

60. This sign means?

A. No parking anytime.

B. Disabled parking spot.

C. No parking here to the corner.

D. No stopping or standing.

61. This sign means?

A. Divided highway ends.

B. Wrong way, turn around.

C. Traffic flows only in the direction of the arrow.

D. Divided highway begins.

62. This sign means?

A. Divided highway ends.

B. Keep to the right of obstruction.

C. Keep to the left of obstruction.

D. Left lane ends.

63. This sign means?

A. Highway exit only.

B. One lane traffic, keep to the right.

C. Traffic is prohibited from entering a restricted roadway.

D. Road closed, construction ahead.

64. This sign means?

A. Right curve warning ahead.

B. Merging traffic entering from the left.

C. Merging traffic entering from the right.

D. 2 Lane traffic ahead.

65. This sign means?

A. Pedestrians only, no vehicle traffic.

B. School advance warning, you are entering a school zone.

C. Pedestrian crossing ahead.

D. Pedestrians ahead warning sign.

66. This warning sign means?

A. Road ramp ahead.

B. Low clearance ahead.

C. Road narrows ahead.

D. Road under water ahead.

67. This sign means?

A. Traffic flows only to the right.

B. Traffic flows only to the left.

C. Your lane will end ahead.

D. Do not drive past this sign, turn around.

68. What type of sign is this?

A. U. S. route sign.

B. County route sign.

C. State route sign.

D. Interstate route sign.

69. This sign means?

A. Completely stop at sign and yield right-of-way traffic.

B. Slow down for an approaching intersection.

C. Slow down, completely stop if required, yield right-of-way traffic.

D. Wrong way, do not enter.

70. This sign means?

A. Church crossing.

B. Pedestrian crossing.

C. Pedestrian traffic only.

D. School crossing.

71. This warning sign means?

A. Right lane ends ahead.

B. Narrow bridge ahead.

C. Left lane ends ahead.

D. Soft shoulder warning ahead.

72. This sign means

    A. Pedestrians only.

    B. Intersection ahead.

    C. Hiking trails ahead.

    D. School crossing ahead.

73. This sign means

    A. Four-lane traffic ahead.

    B. Divided highway ahead.

    C. Two-way traffic ahead.

    D. Intersection ahead.

74. This sign is used to prevent

A. Entrance to full parking lots.

B. Entrance to road construction areas.

C. Entrance to dead-end streets.

D. Wrong-way entrance on one-way streets and expressway ramps.

75. This warning sign means?

A. Stop sign ahead.

B. Reduced speed limit, school zone ahead.

C. School crossing ahead.

D. End of school zone ahead.

76. This sign means?

A. Ski resort ahead.

B. School crossing ahead.

C. Pedestrian crossing ahead.

D. School zone ahead.

77. This exit advisory speed sign means?

   A. Minimum advised speed limit is 25 mph in ideal conditions.

   B. Slow down, maximum advised speed is 25 mph in ideal conditions.

   C. Slow down, maximum advised speed is 25 mph in all conditions.

   D. Minimum advised speed limit is 25 mph in all conditions.

78. This sign means?

   A. General information sign for a bus station.

   B. General information sign for a RV stop.

   C. General information sign for a truck stop.

D. General information sign for a mobile home park.

79. This sign is a warning that you are approaching

    A. An intersection.

    B. A crosswalk.

    C. A railroad crossing.

    D. A blasting zone.

80. This warning sign means?

    A. Left curve ahead warning.

    B. Merging traffic from the right.

    C. Hairpin curve ahead, extreme right curve.

    D. Right turn ahead warning.

81. This sign means

A. Highway changes ahead to the right.

B. Hiking trails ahead to the right.

C. Hotel ahead to the right.

D. Hospital ahead to the right.

82. This sign means?

A. Road workers are in or near the roadway.

B. Snow removal ahead.

C. Pedestrian crossing ahead.

D. Road construction flagger ahead.

TRAFFIC CONTROL
75 QUESTIONS

1. You must notify the DMV within 5 days if you:

    A. Sell or transfer your vehicle.

    B. Fail a smog test for your vehicle.

    C. Get a new prescription for lenses or contacts.

2. You are driving on a one-way street. You may turn left onto another one-way street only if:

    A. A sign permits the turn.

    B. Traffic on the street moves to the right.

    C. Traffic on the street moves to the left.

3. What vehicles must stop at all railroad crossings

    A. Pick up trucks.

    B. School buses and passenger buses carrying passengers.

    C. Motorcycles.

    D. Vehicles towing a trailer.

4. You are driving on a freeway posted for 65 mph. Most of the other vehicles are driving 70 mph or faster. You may legally drive:

A. 70 mph or faster to keep up with the speed of traffic.

B. Between 65 mph and 70 mph.

C. No faster than 65 mph

5. You may drive around or under a gate that is being lowered or raised at a railroad crossing

    A. As long as an approaching train is not too close.

    B. If your vehicle can do so without damaging the gate.

    C. If you first look carefully in both directions.

    D. Under no circumstances.

6. A red and white triangular sign at an intersection means

    A. Slow down if an emergency vehicle is approaching.

    B. Look both ways as you cross the intersection.

    C. Always come to a full stop at the intersection.

    D. Slow down and be prepared to stop if necessary.

7. You come to an intersection which has a flashing red light. You should

   A. Come to a full stop, then go when safe to do so.

   B. Stop only if cars are approaching the intersection.

   C. Stop only if cars are already in the intersection.

   D. Slow down and be prepared to stop if necessary.

8. You see a flashing yellow traffic signal at an upcoming intersection. The flashing yellow light means:

   A. Stop before entering the intersection as long as you can do so safely.

   B. Stop. Yield to all cross traffic before crossing the intersection.

   C. Slow down and cross the intersection carefully.

9. When making a turn, you must _____ your speed.

   A. Increase

   B. Maintain

   C. Vary

D. Reduce

10. When driving on wet roads, you should:

    A. Increase following distance to 5 or 6 seconds

    B. Decrease following distance to 2 seconds

    C. Not be concerned about following distance

    D. Maintain the 4-second following distance rule

11. If a vehicle using high beams comes toward you, you should:

    A. Turn on your high beams

    B. Turn off your headlights

    C. Sound your horn

    D. Flash your high beams

12. Before backing up, you should:

    A. Rely on your mirrors to see if it is clear to proceed

    B. Flash your lights

    C. Open your door to see if it is clear to proceed

D. Turn your head and look through the rear window

13. Unless otherwise posted the speed limit in a residential area is ____.

    A. 20 mph

    B. 25 mph

    C. 30 mph

14. A rectangular-shaped sign is

    A. School crossing sign.

    B. Railroad crossing sign.

    C. Stop sign.

    D. Speed limit sign.

15. Which of the following is true about the speed at which you travel?

    A. The safe speed to drive depends on many conditions

    B. Driving slowly is always safer

    C. The speed limit is always a safe speed

    D. Accelerating is always dangerous

16. You may not cross a single broken white (or yellow) line

    A. When to do so would interfere with traffic.

    B. When turning left into a driveway.

    C. When the car in front is disabled.

    D. When passing to the right on a one-way street.

17. Which of the following is true about driving on a wet roadway?

    A. As you drive faster, your tires become less effective

    B. Water does not affect cars with good tires

    C. Deeper water is less dangerous

    D. As you decrease your speed, the roadway becomes more slippery

18. To help avoid crashes, you should:

    A. Communicate with other drivers on the road

    B. Ignore other drivers on the road

    C. Drive on side streets and back roads

    D. Avoid driving during rush hour

19. When driving on slippery roads, you should:

	A. Use alternate routes

	B. Drive as you would on dry roads

	C. Increase your following distance

	D. Avoid crossing bridges or intersections

20. You have been involved in a minor traffic collision with a parked vehicle and you can`t find the owner. You must:

	A. Leave a note on the vehicle.

	B. Report the accident without delay to the city police or, in unincorporated areas, to the CHP.

	C. Both of the above.

21. If an approaching train is near enough or going fast enough to be a danger, you must

	A. Slow down and proceed with caution.

	B. Not cross the tracks until the train has completely passed.

	C. Cross the tracks at your own risk.

	D. Find an alternative route across tracks.

22. When driving in traffic, it is safest to:

	A. Fluctuate your speed to keep alert

B. Drive faster than the flow of traffic

C. Drive slower than the flow of traffic

D. Drive with the flow of traffic

23. If a traffic signal light is not working, you must:

    A. Stop, then proceed when safe.

    B. Stop before entering the intersection and let all other traffic go first.

    C. Slow down or stop, only if necessary.

24. What can you do to avoid the need to make emergency (or panic) stops while driving in traffic?

    A. Honk your horn to make others aware of your presence

    B. Look ahead and maintain a safe following distance

    C. Drive in the right lane only

    D. Drive slower than the flow of traffic

25. You are approaching a railroad crossing with no warning devices and are unable to see 400 feet down the tracks in one direction. The speed limit is:

    A. 15 mph

    B. 20 mph

    C. 25 mph

26. If an oncoming driver is heading toward you in your lane, you should:

> A. Steer right, blow your horn, and accelerate
>
> B. Steer left, blow your horn, and brake
>
> C. Steer right, blow your horn, and brake
>
> D. Stay in the center of your lane, blow your horn, and brake

27. Before passing another vehicle you should:

> A. Flash your headlights to alert the driver
>
> B. Turn on your four-way flashers to warn the driver
>
> C. Give the proper turn signal to show you are changing lanes
>
> D. Sound your horn to get the drivers attention

28. Before passing another vehicle, you should signal:

> A. Just before changing lanes
>
> B. At any time
>
> C. After changing lanes
>
> D. Early enough so others know your plans

29. With a Class C drivers license a person may drive:

   A. A 3-axle vehicle if the Gross Vehicle Weight is less than 6,000 pounds.

   B. Any 3-axle vehicle regardless of the weight.

   C. A vehicle pulling two trailers.

30. If you are involved in a traffic collision, you are required to complete and submit a written report (SR1) to the DMV:

   A. Only if you or the other driver is injured.

   B. If there is property damage in excess of $750 or if there are any injuries.

   C. Only if you are at fault.

31. When you tailgate other drivers (drive close to their rear bumper):

   A. You can frustrate the other drivers and make them angry.

   B. Your actions cannot result in a traffic citation.

   C. You help reduce traffic congestion.

32. A traffic light which has a green arrow and a red light means that

    A. You may only drive straight ahead.

    B. You may drive only in the direction of the green arrow.

    C. You must wait for a green light.

    D. Vehicles moving in any direction must stop.

33. The amount of space you need to cross traffic depends on the:

    A. Road and weather conditions and oncoming traffic

    B. Presence of a stop sign

    C. Use of your turn signals

    D. Cars behind you

34. What are the colors of a sign which tells you the distance to the next exit of a highway

    A. Yellow with black letters.

    B. Black with white letters.

    C. Red with white letters.

    D. Green with white letters.

35. Drive below the posted speed limit when:

    A. Anything makes conditions less than perfect

    B. Others drive below the speed limit

    C. Entering a highway where there are other cars

    D. You are on a four lane road

36. The most effective thing you can do to reduce your risk of getting injured or killed in a traffic crash is:

    A. Wear your seat belt

    B. Limit your driving to week days

    C. Stay in the right lane on multi-lane highways

    D. Limit your driving to times between 3:00 p.m. and 6:00 p.m.

37. What is the appropriate action to take when approaching a railroad crossing that does not have signals (such as lights or crossing gates)

    A. Always bring the car to a complete stop.

    B. Slow down and be prepared to stop.

    C. Do nothing; all railroad crossings have signals.

D. Increase speed to get across the tracks quickly.

38. A solid white line on the right edge of the highway slants in towards your left. That shows that

    A. There is an intersection just ahead.

    B. You are approaching a construction area.

    C. You will be required to turn left just ahead.

    D. The road will get narrower.

39. When traveling below 40 miles per hour on a limited access highway, you should:

    A. Drive on the shoulder

    B. Use your high beams

    C. Sound your horn to warn others

    D. Use your four-way flashers

40. Your brake lights tell other drivers that you:

    A. Are making a turn

    B. Have your emergency brake on

    C. Are changing lanes

    D. Are slowing down or stopping

41. You may cross a double solid yellow line

    A. To pass a slow moving truck.

    B. To turn into a driveway.

    C. To pass a car if traffic permits.

    D. Under no conditions.

42. You may honk your horn when you:

    A. Have to stop quickly

    B. Are passing another car

    C. Have lost control of your car

    D. Are passing a bicyclist

43. You must obey instructions from school crossing guards:

    A. At all times.

    B. Only during school hours.

    C. Unless you do not see any children present.

44. You may cross a single solid white line in the highway

    A. Whenever you want to.

    B. If traffic conditions require.

    C. Only to turn into a driveway.

D. Only to make a u-turn.

45. What does a flashing yellow light mean

    A. Merging traffic.

    B. Proceed with caution.

    C. Pedestrian crossing.

    D. Come to a full stop.

46. You are driving on a freeway posted for 65 MPH. The traffic is traveling at 70 MPH. You may legally drive:

    A. 70 mph or faster to keep up with the speed of traffic.

    B. Between 65 mph and 70 mph.

    C. No faster than 65 mph.

47. If traffic prevents you from crossing all the way across a set of railroad tracks, you may proceed only when

    A. An approaching train is not moving fast enough to be a danger.

    B. There is room for your vehicle on the other side.

    C. At least one-half of your vehicle can cross the tracks.

    D. No trains are in sight.

48. If you need to slow down or stop when other drivers may not expect it, you should:

    A. Quickly tap your brake pedal a few times

    B. Use your emergency brake

    C. Look over your shoulder for traffic in your blind spot

    D. Get ready to blow your horn

49. At highway speeds, on a dry road, a safe following distance is at least:

    A. 3 seconds of following distance from the car ahead of you

    B. 2 seconds of following distance from the car ahead of you

    C. 4 seconds of following distance from the car ahead of you

    D. 2 car lengths of following distance from the car ahead of you

50. Your blind spot is the area of the road:

    A. You cannot see without moving your head

    B. Directly behind your vehicle

    C. You see in your rearview mirror

    D. You see in your side mirror

51. When driving on wet roads, you should:

    A. Drive the speed limit

    B. Drive slightly faster than the speed limit

    C. Drive 5 to 10 miles below the speed limit

    D. Stay close to the vehicle ahead

52. A diamond-shaped sign is a

    A. Road hazard sign.

    B. Interstate route sign.

    C. School crossing sign.

    D. Speed limit sign.

53. You see a signal person at a road construction site ahead. You should obey his or her instructions:

    A. Only if you see orange cones on the road ahead.

    B. Unless they conflict with existing signs, signals, or laws.

    C. At all times.

54. To prepare for anything coming up in the road ahead, you should:

    A. Continually scan the entire road and roadsides

B. Stare straight ahead at all times

C. Drive with your left foot resting lightly on the brake pedal

D. Maintain focus toward the middle of the road

55. You must use your headlights when other vehicles are not visible from _____ feet away.

    A. 1000

    B. 1500

    C. 1800

    D. 1200

56. When driving on slick roads, you should:

    A. Take turns more slowly

    B. Change lanes quickly

    C. Accelerate quickly

    D. Brake hard

57. If the rear of your vehicle starts to skid left, you should:

    A. Steer left

    B. Hit your brakes

    C. Accelerate

D. Steer right

58. Before changing lanes on a multi-lane highway you should:

    A. Sound your horn

    B. Turn on your headlights

    C. Reduce your speed

    D. Check your mirrors and blind spots

59. An intersection has a stop sign, crosswalk, but no stop line. You must stop

    A. Before the crosswalk.

    B. 50 feet before the intersection.

    C. Where you think the stop line would be.

    D. With your front wheels in the crosswalk.

60. Which of the following must you obey over the other three

    A. A steady red light.

    B. A policeman.

    C. A stop sign.

    D. A flashing red light.

61. Which of these vehicles must always stop before crossing railroad tracks?

> A. Tank trucks marked with hazardous materials placards.
>
> B. Motor homes or pickup trucks towing a boat trailer.
>
> C. Any vehicle with 3 or more axles or weighing more than 4,000 pounds.

62. When the road is marked with a solid yellow line and a broken yellow line on your side you may pass

> A. Only in an emergency.
>
> B. If you are on an expressway.
>
> C. If traffic is clear.
>
> D. Only at an intersection.

63. If a vehicle using high beams comes toward you, you should look towards _____ of the road.

> A. Either side
>
> B. The center
>
> C. The right side
>
> D. The left side

64. Before turning, you should:

    A. Use your signal

    B. Turn the wheel

    C. Increase your speed

    D. Change lanes

65. If your turn signals fail, you should use _____ to indicate you are turning.

    A. Your horn

    B. Your headlights

    C. Hand signals

    D. Your emergency flashers

66. All of the following practices are dangerous to do while driving. Which of these is also illegal?

    A. Listening to music through headphones that cover both ears

    B. Adjusting your outside mirrors.

    C. Transporting an unrestrained animal inside the vehicle.

67. Should you always drive slower than other traffic?

> A. No, you can block traffic when you drive too slowly.
>
> B. Yes, it is a good defensive driving technique.
>
> C. Yes, it is always safer than driving faster than other traffic.

68. As you near an intersection, the traffic light changes from green to yellow. Your best action would be to

> A. Speed up to beat the red light.
>
> B. Apply the brakes sharply to stop.
>
> C. Be prepared to stop in the center of the intersection.
>
> D. Be prepared to stop before the intersection.

69. The safest precaution that you can take regarding the use of cellular phones and driving is:

> A. Use hands-free devices so you can keep both hands on the steering wheel.
>
> B. Keep your phone within easy reach so you won't need to take your eyes off the road.
>
> C. Review the number before answering a call.

70. You should honk your horn when you:

    A. Are travelling through an intersection

    B. Are passing a bicyclist

    C. See a child who is about to run into the street

    D. Are parallel parking

71. When you park on the roadway, you should:

    A. Use your four-way flashers

    B. Park at an angle

    C. Keep your turn signal on

    D. Turn your lights on

72. You just sold your vehicle. You must notify the DMV within ____ days.

    A. 5

    B. 10

    C. 15

73. What are the colors of the warning signs that indicate hazards ahead, such as curves in the road or narrow bridges

    A. Black letters or symbols on a white background.

B. Black letters or symbols on a yellow background.

C. White letters or symbols on a blue background.

D. White letters or symbols on a green background.

74. Which of the following is used on some highways to direct drivers into the proper lanes for turning

    A. Flashing red lights.

    B. Flashing yellow lights.

    C. White lines on the side of the road.

    D. White arrows in the middle of the lanes.

75. Your ability to stop is affected by:

    A. Signal lights

    B. Other cars on the road

    C. The time of day

    D. The condition of the road

SPECIAL DRIVING CONDITION
38 QUESTIONS

1. You want to back out of your driveway. You see children playing nearby. Before you start to move your car you should

    A. Race your motor to warn the children that you are moving.

    B. Sound your horn so the children will hear you.

    C. Walk to the back of the car to be sure the way is clear.

    D. Tell the children to stay away from the driveway.

2. If someone is driving aggressively behind you, you should:

    A. Try to get out of the aggressive driver's way

    B. Stare at the driver as he or she is passing you

    C. Speed up as he or she is passing you

    D. Block the passing lane

3. After an emergency vehicle passes you with its siren on, you must:

> A. Drive closely to the police car
>
> B. Drive as fast as the police car
>
> C. Avoid driving closer than 500 feet behind the emergency vehicle
>
> D. Drive near the curb very slowly

4. When a school bus stops to load or unload children, vehicles traveling in the same direction as the bus must:

> A. Slow down and proceed with caution.
>
> B. Maintain speed.
>
> C. Stop, then proceed with caution.
>
> D. Stop until all persons are clear and the bus moves again.

5. If your car breaks down on a highway, you should:

> A. Sit in your car and wait for help
>
> B. Use your four-way flashers to warn other drivers
>
> C. Sound your horn at passing motorists
>
> D. Flash your headlights at oncoming traffic

6. When you see an emergency vehicle with flashing lights, you must:

   A. Slow down and keep moving in your lane

   B. Keep driving in your lane

   C. Pull to the curb and stop

   D. Stop exactly where you are

7. When driving through a work zone, it is a good safety practice to:

   A. Drive close to the vehicle in front of you to keep traffic flowing freely

   B. Shorten your usual following distance - by about half

   C. Turn on your cruise control

   D. Lengthen your usual following distance - by double

8. A blind person legally has the right-of-way when crossing the street when he is

   A. Wearing light-colored clothing.

   B. Led by a guide dog, or using a white or metallic cane.

   C. Helped by another person.

   D. Wearing dark-colored glasses.

9. A large truck is ahead of you and is turning right onto a street with two lanes in each direction. The truck:

>A. May complete its turn in either of the two lanes.

>B. May have to swing wide to complete the right turn.

>C. Must stay in the right lane at all times while turning.

10. If you begin to feel tired while driving, the best thing to do is:

>A. Get some coffee

>B. Open your window

>C. Stop driving

>D. Turn on the radio

11. If you drive faster than other vehicles on a road with one lane in each direction and continually pass the other cars, you will:

>A. Get you to your destination much faster and safer.

>B. Increase your chances of an accident.

>C. Help prevent traffic congestion.

12. Dim your headlights for oncoming vehicles or when you are within 300 feet of a vehicle:

　　A. You are approaching from behind.

　　B. Approaching you from behind.

　　C. You have already passed.

13. If another driver cuts you off in traffic, you should:

　　A. Pull next to the driver and yell at him or her

　　B. Ignore the other driver

　　C. Flash your high beams at the driver

　　D. Get back at the other driver by cutting him or her off

14. For an average person, how many minutes does the body need to process the alcohol in one drink?

　　A. 15

　　B. 60

　　C. 90

　　D. 30

15. The extra space in front of a large truck is needed for:

　　A. Other drivers when merging onto a freeway.

B. The truck driver to stop the vehicle.

C. Other drivers when they want to slow down.

16. If you have a tire blowout, you should:

    A. Allow the steering wheel to move freely

    B. Let the car slow to a stop

    C. Continue driving until you reach a garage

    D. Brake hard to stop the car immediately

17. Taking drugs along with alcohol:

    A. Increases the risk of causing a crash

    B. Is no more dangerous than alcohol by itself

    C. Lessens the effect of alcohol on your ability to drive

    D. Has no effect on your general driving ability

18. You are driving on the freeway. The vehicle in front of you is a large truck. You should drive:

    A. Closely behind the truck in bad weather because the driver can see farther ahead.

    B. Farther behind the truck than you would for a passenger vehicle.

C. No more than one car length behind the truck so the driver can see

19. Teenagers should try to get at least ___ of sleep each night to avoid the risk of drowsy driving crashes.

    A. 7 hours

    B. 6 hours

    C. 8 hours

    D. 9 hours

20. A pedestrian is crossing your lane but there is no marked crosswalk. You should:

    A. Make sure the pedestrian sees you, but continue driving.

    B. Carefully drive around the pedestrian.

    C. Stop and let the pedestrian cross the street.

21. The effect that lack of sleep has on your safe driving ability is the same as:

    A. The effect that alcohol has

    B. The effect that amphetamines have

    C. The effect that anger has

    D. The effect that driving with teenagers has

22. At intersections, crosswalks, and railroad crossings, you should always:

> A. Stop, listen, and proceed cautiously.
>
> B. Look to the sides of your vehicle to see what is coming.
>
> C. Slowly pass vehicles that seem to be stopped for no reason.

23. When driving on a one way street and an emergency vehicle with flashing lights is behind your car, you:

> A. Drive with your flashers on
>
> B. Drive toward the nearest road side and stop
>
> C. Speed up and take the nearest exit
>
> D. Slow down until the vehicle passes you

24. If another car is in danger of hitting you, you should:

> A. Sound your horn
>
> B. Wave your arms
>
> C. Use your emergency lights
>
> D. Flash your headlights

25. As alcohol builds up in your blood, it:

   A. Slows down your reactions

   B. Makes you feel less confident

   C. Begins to metabolize itself more quickly

   D. Decreases your driving errors

26. If your blood alcohol level is .04, you:

   A. Are 2-7 times more likely to have a crash than a person who has not consumed any

   B. Are above the legal blood alcohol limit but fine to drive

   C. Can be very sure that you will drive safely

   D. Should drink plenty of coffee before getting behind the wheel of your car

27. A motorist approaching a bicyclist should

   A. Speed up to pass him.

   B. Proceed as usual.

   C. Swerve into the opposite lane.

   D. Exercise extreme caution.

28. Motorists should be aware that all bicycles used after dark must have

>A. Reflective handlebar grips.

>B. Front headlight and red taillight.

>C. White reflectors on the front and rear fenders.

>D. Brake lights.

29. When can you drive in a bike lane?

>A. During rush hour traffic if there are no bicyclists in the bike lane.

>B. When you are within 200 feet of a cross street where you plan to turn right.

>C. When you want to pass a driver ahead of you who is turning right.

30. What does a slow moving vehicle emblem look like

>A. A square red sign.

>B. A round green sign.

>C. A diamond-shaped yellow sign.

>D. A triangular orange sign.

31. Crashes in work zones are most commonly the result of:

   A. Tire blow-outs

   B. Hydroplaning because of water sprayed on the roadway

   C. Loss of steering control after driving over wet paint

   D. Carelessness and speeding

32. On a road which has no sidewalks a pedestrian should walk on the

   A. Side of the road which has the lightest traffic.

   B. Same side of the road in which traffic is moving.

   C. Side of the road facing oncoming traffic.

   D. Side of the road which has the heaviest traffic.

33. A motorist should know that a bicyclist operating on a roadway must

   A. Ride on the right side of the road.

   B. Ride on the side of the road facing traffic.

   C. Ride on either side of the road.

D. Ride on the side of the road with the least traffic.

34. There is no crosswalk and you see a pedestrian crossing your lane ahead. You should:

   A. Make eye contact and then pass him/her.

   B. Slow down as you pass him/her.

   C. Stop and let him/her finish crossing the street.

35. _____ limit(s) your concentration, perception, judgment, and memory.

   A. Only a blood alcohol level greater than the legal limit

   B. Alcohol does not

   C. Even the smallest amount of alcohol

   D. Only a blood alcohol level greater than .05

36. A bicyclist differs from a motorist in that he is not required to

   A. Obey the same traffic laws.

   B. Signal all turns.

   C. Report accidents resulting in serious injury.

   D. Insure the bicycle.

37. When you hear a fire engine siren, you must:

>A. Slow down until it passes you

>B. Drive with your flashers on

>C. Pull over to the side of the road and stop

>D. Speed up and take the nearest exit

38. A school bus ahead of you in your lane is stopped with red lights flashing. You should:

>A. Stop, then proceed when you think all of the children have exited the bus.

>B. Slow to 25 MPH and pass cautiously.

>C. Stop as long as the red lights are flashing.

ANSWERS PAGE

General Questions:

1. D 2.C 3.B 4. A 5. D 6. D 7. D 8.C 9.B 10. C

11. A 12.C 13.B 14.A 15.D 16.B 17.C 18.C 19.A 20.D

21. A 22.A 23.A 24.B 25.D 26.D 27.C 28.D 29.A 30.A

31.A 32.A 33.A,B 34.A,B,D 35.B 36.B 37.B,C 38.A 39.A 40.D

41.A,D,F 42.B 43.C 44.A 45.D 46.B 47.B 48.C 49.A 50.B

51.A,B,D 52.A,C,D 53.A 54.C 55.A 56.D 57.B 58.B 59.B 60.B

61.A 62.D 63.A 64.A,C,E 65.B 66.B 67.C 68.C 69.A 70.D

71.D 72.D 73.A,C,D 74.A 75.A,B,E 76.A,B

DEFENSIVE DRIVING

1.A 2.B 3.D 4.C 5.B 6.C 7.B 8.A 9.A 10.D

11.C 12.D 13.A 14.D 15.B 16.B 17.C 18.C 19.C 20.D

21.B 22.D 23.B 24.B 25.A 26.C 27.B 28.C 29.A 30.C

31.A 32.C 33.C 34.D 35.C 36.C 37.A 38.C 39.C 40.A

41.D 42.A 43.B 44.A 45.A 46.A 47.C 48.A 49.A 50.B

51.A 52.D 53.C 54.B 55.A 56.D

ROAD SIGNS

1.C 2.D 3.C 4.D 5.D 6.D 7.B 8.A 9.D 10.B

11.D 12.A 13.C 14.A 15.D 16.A 17.C 18.A 19.B 20.C

21.C 22.C 23.B 24.D 25.B 26.A 27.A 28.A 29.C 30.C

31.C 32.A 33.C 34.A 35.A 36.A 37.D 38.C 39.B 40.C

41.C 42.A 43.C 44.A 45.B 46.A 47.B 48.B 49.B 50.B

51.B 52.C 53.C 54.B 55.B 56.A 57.C 58.A 59.D 60.B

61.C 62.B 63.C 64.C 65.B 66.B 67.D 68.C 69.C 70.D

71.C 72.D 73.C 74.D 75.B 76.C 77.B 78.A 79.C 80.C

81.D 82.A

TRAFFIC CONTROL

1.A 2.C 3.B 4.C 5.D 6.D 7.D 8.C 9.D 10.A

11.D 12.D 13.B 14.D 15.A 16.A 17.A 18.A 19.C 20.C

21.B 22.D 23.A 24.B 25.A 26.C 27.C 28.D 29.A 30.B

31.A 32.B 33.A 34.D 35.A 36.A 37.B 38.D 39.D 40.D

41.B 42.A 43.A 44.B 45.B 46.C 47.B 48.A 49.C 50.A

51.C 52.A 53.C 54.A 55.A 56.A 57.A 58.D 59.A 60.B

61.A 62.C 63.C 64.A 65.C 66.A 67.A 68.D 69.A 70.C

71.A 72.B 73.B 74.D 75.D.

SPECIAL DRIVING CONDITION.

1.C 2.A 3.C 4.D 5.B 6.C 7.D 8.B 9.B 10.C

11.B 12.A 13.B 14.B 15.B 16.B 17.A 18.B 19.C 20.C

21.A 22.B 23.B 24.A 25.A 26.A 27.D 28.B 29.B 30.D

31.D 32.C 33.A 34.C 35.C 36.D 37.C 38.C

Study Guide

With proper preparation you can achieve maximum success in your Massachusetts DMV license test on first sitting.

Having guided many test takers towards achieving success in their DMV exam, I decided to put out this manual which will serve as a standard guide towards helping you pass your DMV.

With this guide there is no need to be afraid of failing as the questions contain there-in are close enough to what you will be tested on.

This test guide is divided into different section of what you will be tested on. The General Question (76), Defensive driving (56), Road signs (82), Traffic Control (75), Special driving condition (38)

With over 300 question and answer in this guide, you are sure of achieving an excellent result at the end of your test.

You are strongly advised to repeat each practical test until you can achieve a consistent score of 90% and above.

Testing Strategy

Prepare yourself to pass your DMV written driver's license test with these simple exam preparation tips.

- Prepare in advance before the test by reading and practicing all included test sections.

- Get a very good night rest prior to the exam.

- Don't spend much time on questions you have no clear answer to. Skip any question you do not understand immediately and return to it later.

- Attend to easy questions first before returning to the hard ones.

- Do not leave any question unanswered; make sure to attend to all questions intelligently.

- Very importantly, study road signs test and know it by heart.

Made in the USA
Middletown, DE
30 November 2019